A Kid's Guide

ALaSKa

"The Last Frontier"

Jack L. Roberts
Michael Owens

Curious Kids Press • Palm Springs, CA
www.curiouskidspress.com

Publisher: *Curious Kids Press, Palm Springs, CA 92264.*
Designed by: *Michael Owens*
Editor: *Sterling Moss*
Copy Editor: *Janice Ross*

Table of Contents

A WORD TO PARENTS

CURIOUS KIDS PRESS is passionate about helping young readers expand and enhance their understanding about countries and cultures around the world. While actual real-world experiences with other countries and cultures may have the most profound positive effect on children and pre-teens, we understand such experiences are not always possible. That's why our two series of books — "A Kid's Guide to . . ." (for ages 9-12) and "Let's Visit . . ." (for ages 6-8) — are designed to bridge that gap and help young readers explore the wonderful world of diversity in everything from food and holidays to geography and traditions. We hope your young explorers enjoy this adventure into the 49th U.S. state, Alaska.

Chapter 1

Welcome to Alaska

Alaska's marine animals include sea otters, porpoises and dolphins, harbor seals, and these magnificent creatures—humpback whales. (See page 44.)

WHAT'S THERE FOR KIDS TO DO in Alaska?

Are you kidding? Lots of things!

From bear watching to whale watching...from gold mining to dog sledding (or dog mushing—the official state sport).

And that's just for starters.

So, what are you waiting for? Turn the page to learn more about awesome Alaska—the 49th state of the United States of America.

Alaska At-a-Glance

Name: Alaska

Capital City: Juneau

Total Area (Size): 663,268 sq. miles (1,717,856 sq. km); (more than twice as big as the state of Texas)

Population: 731,545 (smaller than the population of Indianapolis, Indiana)

Official Language: English and more than a dozen other languages, some spoken by fewer than 100 people

State Motto: "North to the Future." It means Alaska is a land of promise.

Admitted to the Union: January 3, 1959 (49th state)

The Alaska Flag

In 1926, the Territory of Alaska held a contest for students to design a new flag for the territory. A thirteen-year-old Alaskan boy named Benny Benson decided to enter the contest.

Benny designed a flag with a blue field. He said it represented the sky and the Forget-Me-Not, the state flower. He added the North Star, which represented the future of the state of Alaska. Finally, Benny's design included the Big Dipper, which, he said, stood for strength.

Benny's flag design won—out of more than 700 entries. His design was adopted as the official flag for the Territory of Alaska. Later, it became the official flag of the State of Alaska.

Alaska's State Seal

Alaska's state seal is designed to tell about this huge state.

- The rays above the mountains represent the Northern Lights.
- The train stands for Alaska's railroads.
- The ships stand for transportation by sea.
- The trees symbolize Alaska's wealth of forests.
- The farmer and his horse represent Alaskan agriculture.
- The fish and the seals signify the importance of fishing and wildlife to Alaska's economy.

Where in the World is Alaska?

ALASKA IS THE U.S. STATE that is farthest north. (Hawaii is farthest south.) It borders the Canadian province of British Columbia on the east, the Arctic Ocean in the north, the Bering Sea in the west, and the Pacific Ocean and Gulf of Alaska in the south.

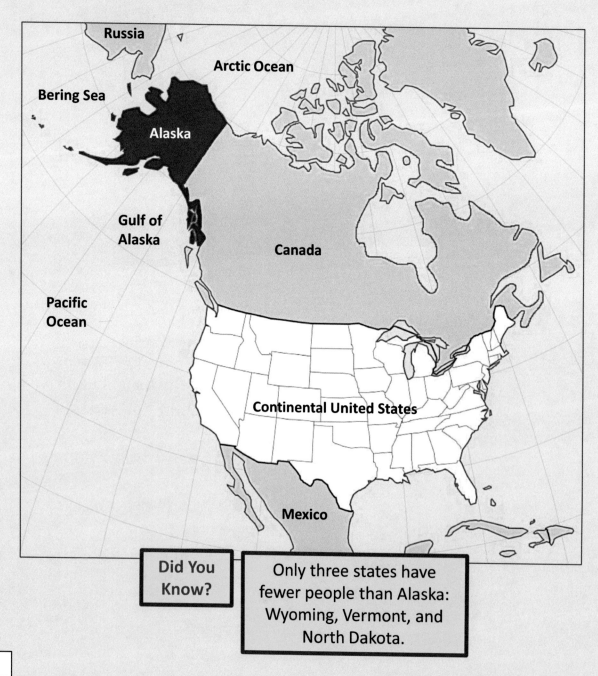

Russia

Arctic Ocean

Bering Sea

Alaska

Gulf of Alaska

Pacific Ocean

Canada

Continental United States

Mexico

Did You Know?

Only three states have fewer people than Alaska: Wyoming, Vermont, and North Dakota.

THe Size OF ALaSKa

ALASKA IS BIG! Really big! It's about one-fifth as large as all of the continental United States. It is also twice as big as Texas, the second largest state in the Union.

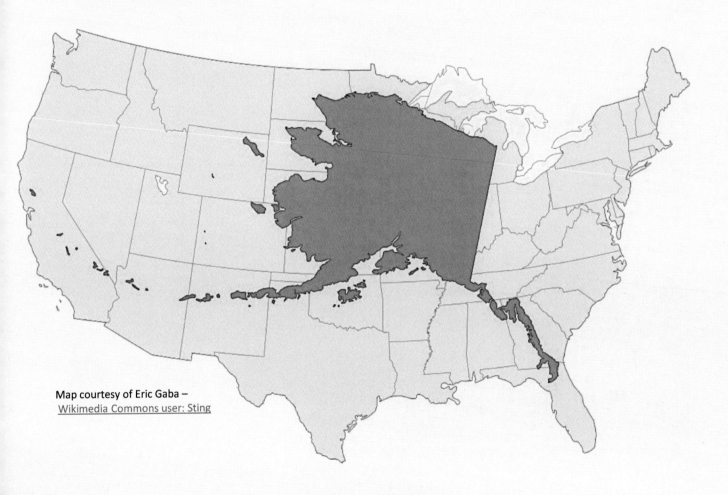

Map courtesy of Eric Gaba –
Wikimedia Commons user: Sting

How Big Is Alaska?

Here are 4 ways to think about it.

- Alaska is more than three times as big as the country of France.

- If Alaska were a country, it would be the 17th largest country in the world.

- Alaska is bigger than Texas, California, and Montana combined.

- 428 states the size of Rhode Island could fit in Alaska.

Cool Facts About Alaska

The name "Alaska" comes from the Aleut word "Alaxsxaq" (also spelled Aleyska"). It means "great land" or "mainland."

The Third Largest Lake
In the United States

Lake Iliamna in Alaska is the third largest lake in the United States. It measures 1,150 square miles (2,978 sq. km). That makes it only slightly smaller than the U.S. state of Rhode Island.

The tall, stately Sitka spruce is the state tree. It is found in southeastern and central Alaska.

Strange But True
More caribou (aka reindeer) live in Alaska than people.
Caribou: 1,000,000 +
People: 731,545

Juneau (the capital)
There are no roads that connect Juneau, the capital of Alaska, to any other part of Alaska. You can get to Juneau only by boat or plane.

Almost half of Alaska's land is tundra. That's land where no large trees can grow.

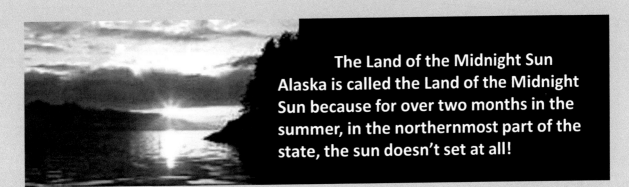

The Land of the Midnight Sun
Alaska is called the Land of the Midnight Sun because for over two months in the summer, in the northernmost part of the state, the sun doesn't set at all!

The Yukon River in Alaska is one of the longest rivers in the United States. The river is 1,980 miles (3,190 km) long. It starts in British Columbia, Canada and flows through the Canadian Yukon Territory for about 714 miles (1,150 km).

ALASKA BY-THE-NUMBERS

70 (or more)
The number of active **volcanoes** in Alaska.

Mount Cleveland

100,000
The number of **glaciers** in Alaska.

Taku Glacier

12,000
The number of **rivers, streams, and creeks.**

Yukon River

17 million
Number of acres of the Tongass National Forest.

Forest path

280,000
The **population of Anchorage**, Alaska's largest city.

Downtown Anchorage

24,000
The average number of yearly **earthquakes!**

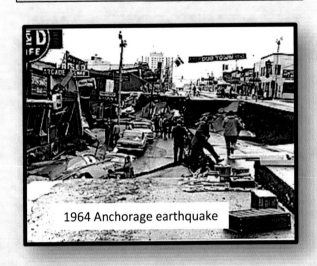
1964 Anchorage earthquake

200 feet
Average **height of the Sitka spruce**, Alaska's State Tree.

Sitka Spruce

20,310 feet
The **tallest mountain peak** in Alaska in Denali National Park.

Denali

A Brief History of Alaska

20,000 to 6,000 BCE

First humans migrate from Siberia across a land bridge into parts of Alaska.

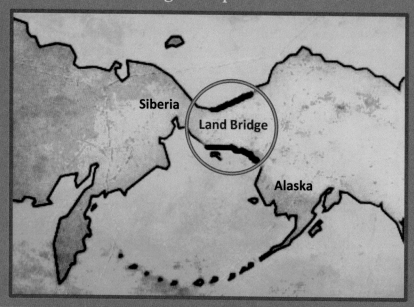

1741

The first European steps foot on Alaska soil.

1804

Russians defeat Alaskan Natives and establish a permanent Russian settlement at Sitka.

1867

The United States buys Alaska from Russia for $7.2 million. (That's the same as about $109 million in 2018.)

1897-1900

Klondike gold rush in Yukon Territory produces heavy traffic through Alaska on the way to the gold fields.

1907 U.S. President Theodore Roosevelt establishes the Tongass National Forest.

1916

First bill proposing Alaska statehood is introduced in Congress.

1959

President Dwight Eisenhower signs statehood measure on January 3, making Alaska the 49th State.

1973

The first Iditarod Trail Sled Dog Race begins on March 3. (See page 16.)

2006

Voters elect the state's first female governor.

Chapter 2

People Customs, and Traditions

PEOPLE HAVE LIVED in Alaska for thousands of years.

These first Alaskans were made up of three different groups: Eskimos (including Inuit), Indians, and Aleuts. Within these three groups, there are many different cultures and languages.

Today, the Eskimo people live in Greenland and Canada, as well as Alaska.

Among the Eskimos, there are the Yupik (pronounced *you-pik*) Eskimos of Southwestern Alaska and Inuit (pronounced *i-noo-it*) Eskimos of the far north.

In Canada and Greenland, the Inuit prefer to be called Inuit. The term Eskimo is considered negative or insulting.

Yet, in Alaska, many **descendants** of the original people there still prefer the term Eskimo.

The three different groups of Alaska Natives live in different parts of Alaska. Look at the map below. It shows where these three groups live today.

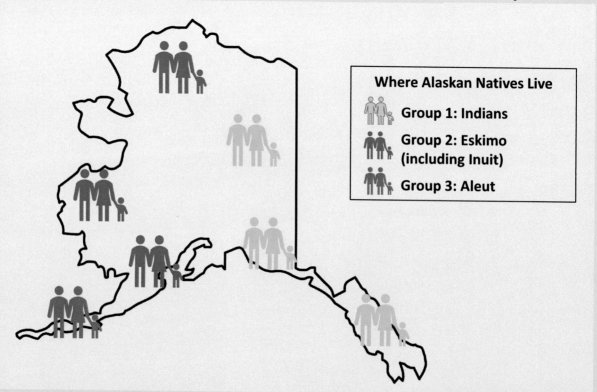

Seward's Folly
The Story of the Purchase of Alaska

William H. Seward

IN THE MID 1860's, Russia owned a huge territory in North America, known as Russian American. The territory included land we now call Alaska.

William H. Seward, the U.S. Secretary of State at the time, thought the U.S. should buy the territory. He wanted to expand the size of the United States.

The purchase price was $7.2 million. That was only about two cents an acre. But many people thought the purchase was ridiculous. They didn't think the land had any real value. They called the purchase Seward's Folly.

Nevertheless, in 1867 the Senate finally voted in favor of the purchase—by one vote! Nearly 100 years later, on January 3, 1959, Alaska became the 49th state of the United States.

So, did Seward make a good investment for the United States?

Seward's Day
Every year, on the last Monday in March, Alaska celebrates Seward's Day. It's a day to remember and honor the purchase of Alaska from Russia in 1867.

The Iditarod Trail Sled Dog race

WHO HAS THE BEST sled dog team in the world?

Every March in Alaska, there is a nearly 1,000-mile (1,600-meter) race to find out. It's called the Iditarod Trail Sled Dog race, which runs from Anchorage to Nome.

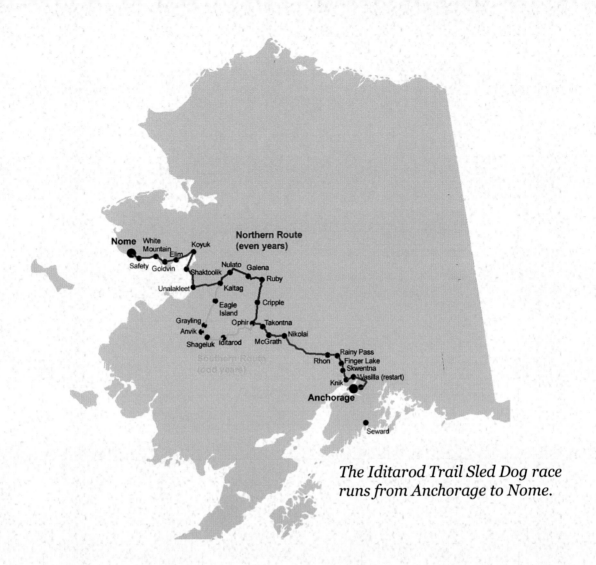

The Iditarod Trail Sled Dog race runs from Anchorage to Nome.

Mushers each have a team of 14 dogs and cover the route in anywhere from 8 to fifteen days (or more). In 2017, a musher broke the record for the fastest time when he crossed the finish line in Nome in 8 days, 3 hours, 40 minutes, and 13 seconds.

The Iditarod began in 1973. It was designed to test the best sled dog mushers and teams. But it is also meant to honor the relay race in 1925 that brought life-saving medicine to Nome during an epidemic of diphtheria. (See page 18.)

(See page 18.)

Who Won the 1978 Race? You Decide!

In 1978, two mushers finished the Iditarod race almost at the exact same time.

The nose of Musher 1's lead dog crossed the finish line first.

But...

The body of Musher 2 crossed the finish line first.

So, who do you think won the race? Musher 1 or Musher 2? Find out on page 46.

Balto
A Beloved and Heroic Sled Dog

A bronze statue of Balto stands in Central Park in New York City near the Tisch Children's Zoo.

IN JANUARY 1925, a terrible disease, called diphtheria, was quickly spreading through the town of Nome, Alaska. The only medicine that could stop the disease was in Anchorage, Alaska. But there were no roads directly from Anchorage to Nome.

To make matters worse, there was only one airplane in Anchorage that could get the medicine to Nome. But its engine was frozen.

Officials finally decided there was only one way to get the medicine to Nome. That was by dogsled.

First, it was taken by train to the town of Nenana, 674 miles (1,085 km) from Nome. Then, a series of dogsled teams headed out in a relay as fast as they could with the medicine.

More than 20 dogsled teams and their mushers moved the medicine in blizzard conditions from Nenana to Nome. Freezing temperatures along the route reached as low as −62 °F (−52 °C).

The last leg of the trip was led by a six-year-old Siberian Husky named Balto. As soon as he arrived in Nome with the medicine, Balto was hailed a hero. He became a celebrity.

In December of that year, a statue of Balto was erected in New York City's Central Park, where it still stands in his memory today.

The Rest of the Story
"The Most Heroic Animal Of All Time"

Balto deserves a great deal of credit. But there was another Siberian Husky who contributed even more to the race to Nome. His name was Togo. Togo ran more than 250 miles (402 km) in the relay race. Balto ran only the last 30 miles (48 km). In 2011, *Time* magazine recognized Togo for his courage and what he achieved. The magazine named Togo "the most heroic animal of all time."

AN Imaginary Interview With AN Inuit

THERE ARE MANY DIFFERENT GROUPS of Alaska Natives—the **indigenous** (or original) people of Alaska. The largest group is the Inuit. Today, there are about 55,000 Inuit people living in Alaska.

From the earliest days, the Inuit learned to survive in a very harsh, cold climate. They developed a special, unique culture. In their culture, for example, people were expected to help others and share the wealth.

Today, most Inuit live in modern homes. Some still hunt and fish for a living. But others work in the same traditional jobs as everyone else.

Would you like to know more about these special people? To get started, here is an imaginary conversation with one Inuk man.

What does Inuit mean?

The word means "the people." If you're talking about one person, the word is "Inuk."

What's the difference between Inuit and Eskimo?

The word Eskimo does not come from any native Alaskan language. It was a name given to us by outsiders. Some native Alaskans don't mind it. But the Inuit people generally prefer the name Inuit. They find the word Eskimo insulting.

Do Inuit people still live in igloos?

The Inuit are famous for their igloos. But today, they are mostly used as a temporary shelter during winter hunting trips. BTW, the word igloo means any place where people live. So you could live in a mansion or in a mobile home and still live in an igloo.

What do Inuits eat and drink?

Food. (LOL) In the past, the Inuit ate mostly meat from hunting. It's hard to grow food in the Arctic. Today, we eat a lot of traditional store-bought products.

What are some things Inuit invented?

The Inuit invented many useful things to help them survive in the freezing environment. For example, they invented the kayak for one person to use for hunting the ocean. They also invented the harpoon, which was used to hunt seals and whales. They invented snowshoes with "spikes" (made from caribou bone) on the bottom to help grip the snow and ice.

CHAPTER 3

Landmarks and Attractions

WHAT ARE THE THREE THINGS that kids who visit Alaska want to see most? Glacier, glaciers, and more glaciers. In fact, glaciers top the list of things visitors of all ages want to see when visiting Alaska.

And, for sure, Alaska is home to some of the most awesome glaciers in the world. They range in depth from a few dozen feet thick to over 4,500 feet (1,371 m).

But there are many other fun things to do and see in Alaska. Here are just a few of the awesome landmarks and attractions in "the Frontier State."

Glacier Bay National Park

EVERY YEAR, MORE THAN 600,000 PEOPLE from around the world visit Glacier Bay National Park in Alaska. They come for many reasons— great outdoor recreation, amazing scenery, and spectacular wildlife, including brown bears, mountain goats, whales, and much more.

But they also come to visit the world's most awesome glaciers.

The park is more than three million acres in size. That's about the size of the U.S. state of Connecticut.

There are more than 1,000 glaciers in Glacier Bay. Seven are known as tidewater glaciers. That's a glacier that flows all the way down the mountain to the ocean.

Margerie Glacier

ONE OF THE MOST IMPRESSIVE tidewater glaciers in Glacier Bay National Park is called the Margerie Glacier. It is about 21 miles (34 km) long and 1 mile (1.6 km) wide. It is about 250 feet (76 m) high. The base of the glacier is 100 feet (30 m) underwater.

Most of the tidewater glaciers in the park have been retreating over the last several decades. A retreating glacier isn't moving backwards. It is just melting faster than gaining new ice.

Margerie Glacier is different. It is advancing (or growing). It flows about six feet (1.8 m) per day.

What is a glacier?

A glacier is a thick mass of ice that covers a large area of land. It forms when snow doesn't melt during the summer months. Over hundreds of years, the snow builds up. It turns into solid ice—a glacier.

The weight of a glacier causes it to move slowly downhill. Some glaciers move only a few feet a year. Others move more quickly, often several feet every day.

Quick Quiz

There are glaciers in mountain ranges on every continent except one. Can you guess which one that is? Hint: It's also a country. **Answer: Australia**

THe NORTH POLe

KIDS ALL OVER THE WORLD have heard about the North Pole. It's often said to be the home of Santa Claus and his reindeer.

So, where exactly is the North Pole?

The North Pole is the northernmost point of Earth. It is directly opposite the South Pole in Antarctica. It is located in the middle of the Arctic Ocean—not exactly a good place for Santa's Workshop.

But there is another North Pole—North Pole, Alaska. It's a small town about 1,700 miles (2,700 km) south of Earth's geographic North Pole.

But that doesn't matter.

Today, kids of all ages (and adults, too!) love to visit North Pole, Alaska. There's a gift shop named Santa Claus House. Outside, there is a large statue of Santa Claus. People love to have their picture taken with the giant Santa Claus.

And every December, the post office in North Pole receives hundreds of thousands of letters addressed to Santa Claus at 1 Santa Claus Lane, North Pole, Alaska.

Alaska Train

WHO DOESN'T LOVE a train ride? And in Alaska, there are many different opportunities for train trips throughout the state on the Alaska Railroad.

For example, try the Fairbanks Family Fun Train. It's a two-and-a-half-hour round-trip journey. That's plenty of time to enjoy family-friendly games, crafts and snacks while taking in sweeping views of Alaska's amazing land.

Or, if you are there in October, try the Kids' Halloween Train. There's entertainment from a magician, crafts, balloon animals, Halloween-themed Bingo, a raffle and coloring contest. It's a "Spooktacular" time for all.

Denali National Park & Preserve

DENALI NATIONAL PARK & PRESERVE is where you'll find the tallest mountain peak in North America. Today, that mountain is called Denali. But for many years it was known as Mount McKinley. (*See page 30.*)

But there is more to do at the Denali National Park than just gaze at this amazing mountain—from hiking to biking to camping to visiting a sled dog kennel.

The park was established in 1917. At the time, the purpose was to protect Dall sheep from being hunted too much.

Today, the park has grown to about 6 million acres (about 9,375 square miles or 24,281 sq km). That's about the size of the state of New Hampshire.

More than 400,000 people from around the world visit the park each year. They come to see the spectacular scenery and the vast wilderness. They also come to see the animals—bears, moose, fox, Dall sheep, caribou, wolves, and more.

Fun Fact
Denali National Park has only one road and only one road entrance. The road is 92 miles (148 km) long. The park is only 300 miles south of the Arctic Circle.

Science Fact
Did you know that sled dogs have two different kinds of fur? On the outside of their coats, there is a layer of fur called "guard hairs." This layer acts like a water-resistant rain jacket. There is also a layer of fur underneath. This fur acts like a warm fleece jacket. With these two different kinds of fur, sled dogs stay warm in the extremely cold winter temperatures in Denali.

Denali
(Formerly Mt. McKinley)

Denali
At-a-Glance

Height: 20,310 feet (6, 190 m)

Lowest Temperature Recorded: Approximately −100 °F (−73 °C)

First Ascent: June 7, 1913

First Woman to Reach Summit: 1947

First Descent on Skis: 1972 by extreme skier Sylvain Saudan, known as "Skier of the Impossible."

FOR NEARLY 100 YEARS, the highest mountain peak in North America was known to most people in the United States and around the world as Mount McKinley. It was named after president-elect William McKinley in 1896, even though McKinley had no direct connection to the mountain.

A few years later, in 1917, Mt. McKinley National Park was established. It was the first national park created specifically to protect wildlife.

Yet, from the beginning, many people objected to the name. They felt this amazing mountain should have a Native Alaskan name.

Native Alaskans had lived around the mountain for centuries. They called the peak Denali, a word that mean "high" or "tall."

Finally, in 2015, the U.S. government officially changed the name to Denali.

Today, Denali National Park and Preserve consists of six million acres. That's larger than the state of New Hampshire. Wild animals, large and small, roam the unfenced lands.

Sitka National Historic Park/ Totem Park

TAKE A WALK along the Totem Trail at Sitka National Historic Park/Totem Park. The park is located on a beautiful small island about 95 miles (150 km) southwest of Juneau, the capital of Alaska. It's the site where the Russian traders and the Tlingit Indians fought a fierce battle in 1804.

In 1890, a federal park was established in Sitka as a remembrance to this battle. Totem poles were installed along a trial through the park. The poles were gifts from native Tlingit and Haida chiefs.

Today, there are 20 totem poles. Each has a different story carved in it. Together, the poles tell a story of Native cultures in this coastal region of Alaska.

The park also includes a **temperate rain forest** and beach area. During the summer you can go on a Ranger-led Totem Walk to learn about the history of Sitka, the park, and the totem poles.

Chapter 4

The Animals of Alaska

NEARLY 1000 DIFFERENT VERTEBRATE SPECIES live in the state of Alaska. They range from bears and mountain goats to whales and seals to birds and reptiles.

Holding a special spot among all these animals is the **Moose.** On May 1, 1998, the moose became the official land mammal of Alaska.

On the next pages, you can read about the moose and some of the other special animals of Alaska.

Don't call us meese!

Or mooses. We're just moose, even if there is a bunch of us together.

Moose cow and calf

MOOSE
At-a-Glance

Height: Up to 6 feet tall.

Weight: From about 800 pounds (female) to 1,600 pounds (male).

Lifespan: Rarely more than 16 years.

Diet: Herbivorous: Willow, birch, and aspen twigs in winter; leaves of birch, willow, and aspen in summer.

Other: The moose (or elk as it is called in Europe) is the largest member of the deer family.

Brown Bear

IF YOU WANT TO SEE a brown bear in the wild, a good place to go is Alaska. Nearly all brown bears in the United States live in Alaska and can be found throughout the state.

According to experts, brown bears are extremely intelligent. (That doesn't mean a brown bear can add 2 + 2, of course.) Each one also has its own unique or special personality.

Brown bears have a very good sense of smell, even better than most dogs. Their eyesight and hearing are also very good.

Brown bears can be fun to watch. But be careful. They can also be very dangerous.

BROWN BEAR (aka GRIZZLY BEAR)
At-a-Glance

Length: Up to 9 ft 2 in (2.8 m)

Height (at the shoulder): Up to 5 ft (153 cm).

Weight: 400 lbs (180 kg) on average.

Lifespan: 25 years on average.

Diet: Omnivorous (eats everything from berries and honey to meat).

Other: Claws grow up to 4 inches (10 cm) long.

"Bear-Ware"
Alaska Is Bear Country
A Quick Quiz

Bears are probably the most frequently seen wild animals in Alaska. They are found in the wild, but also in many cities, rummaging through garbage dumpsters.

How much do you know about the three different species of bears in Alaska. Let's find out.

Read each statement below. Decide if it is true or false. On the line provided, write T for True or F for False. Check your answers on page 46.

1. Brown bears are poor swimmers.

_____

2. Brown bears can run in short bursts up to 40 mph (64 kph).

_____

3. The lifespan of a polar bear is about 25 years.

_____

4. The polar bear is the smallest of the three bears.

_____

5. There are more polar bears in Alaska than any other bear.

_____

Dall Sheep

WHAT'S THE FIRST THING you notice about Dall Sheep? Probably their huge curled horns. They're stunning. And beautiful.

Dall sheep live on the rugged cliffs and peaks of mountains in central and northern Alaska. The rugged land helps them avoid **predators** who can't climb as well as Dall sheep, who rarely fall from the cliffs.

Adult rams (males) live together. They don't mix with ewe (female) groups except to mate in late November and early December.

DALL SHEEP
At-a-Glance

Height: 3 feet (.91 m) at the shoulder.

Weight: Up to 180 pounds (81 kilograms).

Lifespan: Rams (males) up to 16 years; ewes (females) up to 19 years.

Diet: Herbivorous (grasses, moss, other plants)

Predators: Wolves, coyotes, brown bears

Other: The age of a Dall sheep can be determined by the pattern of rings, called annuli, spaced along the length of the horn.

Bald Eagle

THE BALD EAGLE is the national emblem of the United States. It was chosen in 1782 for its long life, great strength, and majestic looks.

Today, there is an estimated 30,000 bald eagles in Alaska. That's more than anywhere else in the United States.

BALD EAGLE
At-a-Glance

Weight: Between 8 to 14 pounds (3.6 to 6.4 kg).

Length: 28-40 inches (70-102 cm).

Wingspan: Up to 7.5 feet (2.3 m).

Lifespan: Around 20 years in the wild; somewhat longer in captivity.

Diet: Mainly fish.

Other: It was named by the early American colonists. At that time, the word "bald" (or "balled") meant white, not hairless.

Caribou

IN EUROPE, THEY ARE CALLED REINDEER, even though reindeer and caribou are the same animal. But, of course, singing "Rudolph the red-nosed caribou" just doesn't sound right, does it!

Caribou are the only members of the deer family in which both males and females grow antlers.

In Alaska, there are 32 different groups of caribou. Like most herd animals, caribou travel great distances to find food—up to 400 miles (640 km) between their summer and winter ranges.

CARIBOU
At-a-Glance

Shoulder Height): 33 to 59 in. (85 to 150 cm)

Weight (male): Up to 400 lbs (182 kg); (female) up to 225 lbs (120 kg).

Lifespan (in the wild): 15 years.

Population: Approximately 750,000 in Alaska

Diet: Herbivore.

Predators: Bears and Wolves

Humpback Whale

The Whale Acrobats of the World

Did You Know?

Humpback whales don't actually have a hump on their backs. So, why are they called humpback? When they dive into the ocean, their backs form an arch. It looks like a hump.

THERE ARE FOURTEEN DIFFERENT SPECIES (or kinds) of whales that make their home (at least part of the year) in the waters around Alaska, including the Killer whale and the Blue whale.

But one of the most interesting whales is the humpback for two reasons.

First, they are acrobats. They perform what is called a "fluke up dive." They **propel** themselves from the water and dive back in.

They also slap the water with their flippers, which can be up to 16 feet (5 m) long. That's almost half as long as the average yellow school bus.

Humpback whales also "sing." All males in a group sing the same song. Whales in the North Atlantic sing one song. Whales in the North Pacific sing another. A typical song lasts ten to twenty minutes. Both groups repeat the same song for hours at a time.

Humpback whales around Alaska spend the summer in Glacial Bay. They then swim to Hawaii for the winter. It's not an easy trip (or migration). It is 6,000 miles (9,656 km) and takes six to eight weeks.

Humpback whales are huge. But they are not the biggest whales in the sea. That title goes to the blue whale. It can weigh twice as much as the humpback.

HUMPBACK WHALE
At-a-Glance
Length: Up to 49 feet (14.9 m).
Weight: 35 tons. (An adult African elephant weighs only about 6 tons.)
Lifespan: 40-50 years.
Population: 60,000 worldwide; only about 5,000 in Alaskan waters during the summer.
Diet: Krill and other small fish.

Glossary

Ascent (*noun*): The act of climbing up.

Culture (*noun*): The language, ideas, customs, beliefs, and art of a particular group of people.

Descendant (*noun*): Someone who is related to a person or group of people who lived in the past.

Indigenous (*adjective*): A word that refers to the very first people to live in an area.

Investment (*noun*): Money or property put to use in a way that will result in a profit (or additional money).

Land Bridge (*noun*): A connection between two landmasses.

Mammal (*noun*): A warm-blooded animal that feeds its babies with milk from the mother.

Predator (*noun*): An animal that lives by killing and eating other animals.

Species (noun): In biology, a group of animals or plants that are similar and can produce young animals or plants.

Symbolize (*verb*): To stand for or represent.

Temperate Rainforest: A forest found mainly near coastal areas that gets lots of rain, fog, and mist, and is cooler than a tropical rainforest

Vertebrate (*noun*): In biology, an animal that has a backbone.

ANSWER: Who Won the 1978 Iditarod Race?

Musher 1. You might say he won by a nose.

"Bear-Ware"
Answers from Page 37

1. False. They are excellent swimmers.

2. True.

3. True.

4. False. The black bear is the smallest of the three bears.

5. False. Black bears are the most abundant. There is an estimated 100,000 black bears in Alaska.

An Important New Book
For All Young Readers
And Their Families

Curious Kids Press

A Kid's Guide to
CLiMate CHaNge
And Global WarMing

Jack L. Roberts
Michael Owens

Available on amazon.com

Explore the World

Find these books on Amazon.com
Preview them at curiouskidspress.com

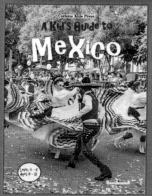
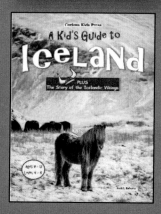

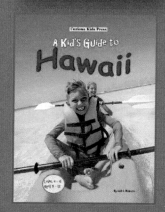
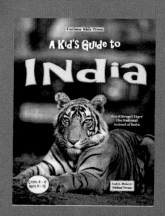

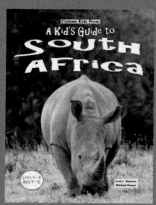

A Kid's Guide to
ALaSKa
For Parents and Teachers

About This Book

A Kid's Guide to . . . is an engaging, easy-to-read book series that provides an exciting adventure into fascinating countries and cultures around the world for young readers. Each book focuses on one country, continent, or U.S. territory or state, and includes colorful photographs, informational charts and graphs, and quirky and bizarre "Did You Know" facts, all designed to bring the country and its people to life. Designed primarily for recreational, high-interest reading, the informational text series is also a great resource for students to use to research geography topics or writing assignments.

About the Reading Level

A Kid's Guide to . . . is an informational text series designed for kids in grades 4 to 6, ages 9 to 12. For some young readers, the series will provide new reading challenges based on the vocabulary and sentence structure. For other readers, the series will review and reinforce reading skills already achieved. While for still other readers, the book will match their current skill level, regardless of age or grade level.

About the Authors

Jack L. Roberts began his career in educational publishing at Children's Television Workshop (now Sesame Workshop), where he was Senior Editor of The Sesame Street/Electric Company Reading Kits. Later, at Scholastic Inc., he was the founding editor of a high-interest/low-reading level magazine for middle school students. He also founded two technology magazines for teachers and administrators.

Roberts is the author of more than two dozen biographies and other nonfiction titles for young readers, published by Scholastic Inc., the Lerner Publishing Group, Teacher Created Materials, Benchmark Education, and others.. More recently, he was the co-founder of WordTeasers, an educational series of card decks designed to help kids of all ages improve their vocabulary through "conversation, not memorization."

Michael Owens is a noted jazz dance teacher, award-winning wildlife photographer, graphic arts designer, and devoted animal lover.

In 2017, Roberts and Owens launched Curious Kids Press (CKP), an educational publishing company focused on publishing high-interest, nonfiction books for young readers, primarily books about countries and cultures around the world. Currently, CKP has published two series of country books: "A Kid's Guide to..." (for ages 9-12 and "Let's Visit . . ." (for ages 6-8) — both designed to help young readers explore the wonderful world of diversity in everything from food and holidays to geography and traditions.

To Our Valued Customers

Curious Kids Press is passionate about creating fun-to-read books about countries and cultures around the world for young readers, and we work hard every day to create quality products.

All of our books are Print on Demand books. As a result, on rare occasions, you may find minor printing errors. If you feel you have not received a quality printed product, please send us a description and photo of the printing error along with your name and address and we will have a new copy sent to you free of charge. Contact us at: info@curiouskidspress.com

Made in the USA
Las Vegas, NV
26 June 2023